San Diego

JEWEL OF THE CALIFORNIA COAST

by Charlene Baldridge

NORTHLAND PUBLISHING

Contents

Oceanside
Carlsbad
Escondido
Encinitas
Del Mar
Torrey Pines
La Jolla
Mission Bay
SeaWorld
San Diego
Coronado
Imperial Beach
Tijuana

PACIFIC OCEAN

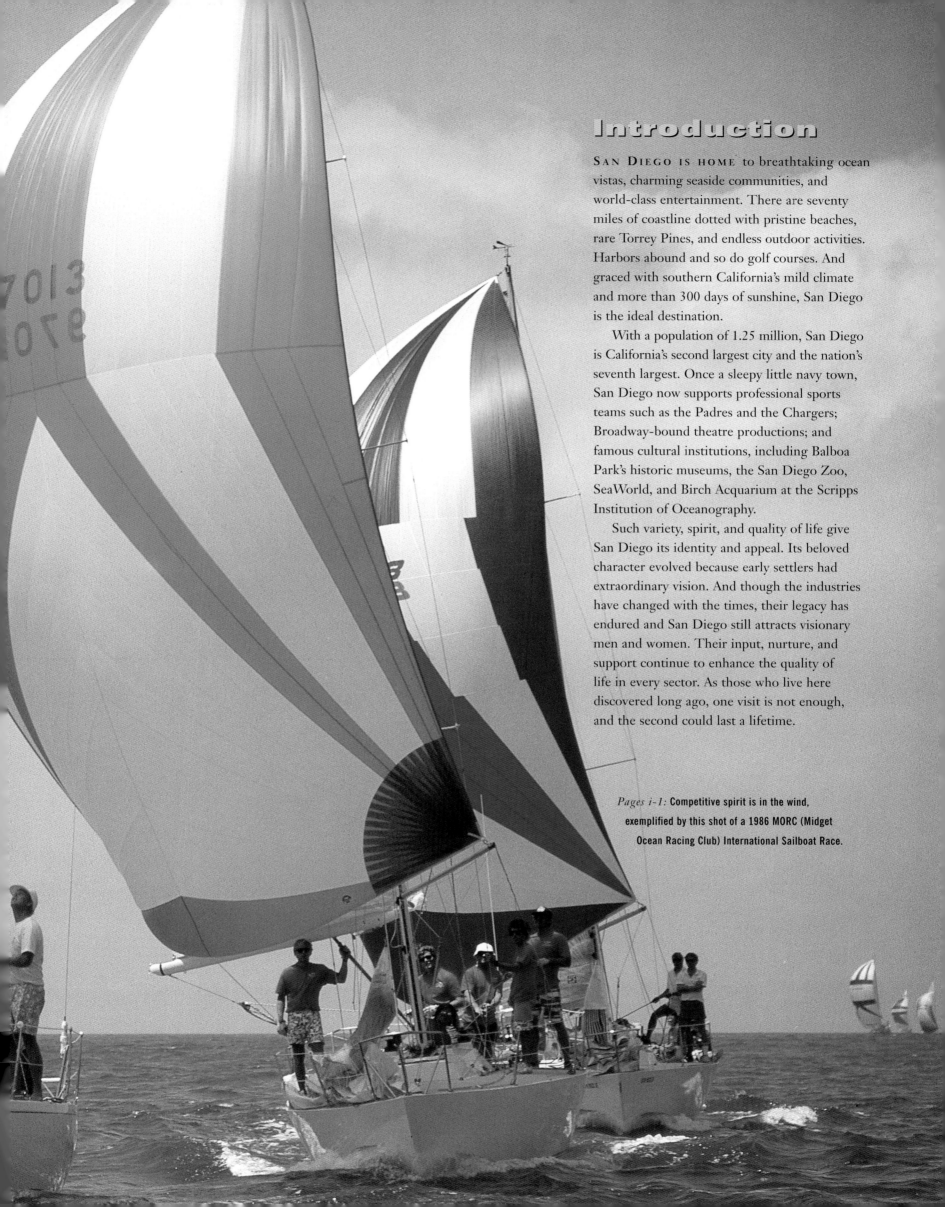

Introduction

SAN DIEGO IS HOME to breathtaking ocean vistas, charming seaside communities, and world-class entertainment. There are seventy miles of coastline dotted with pristine beaches, rare Torrey Pines, and endless outdoor activities. Harbors abound and so do golf courses. And graced with southern California's mild climate and more than 300 days of sunshine, San Diego is the ideal destination.

With a population of 1.25 million, San Diego is California's second largest city and the nation's seventh largest. Once a sleepy little navy town, San Diego now supports professional sports teams such as the Padres and the Chargers; Broadway-bound theatre productions; and famous cultural institutions, including Balboa Park's historic museums, the San Diego Zoo, SeaWorld, and Birch Acquarium at the Scripps Institution of Oceanography.

Such variety, spirit, and quality of life give San Diego its identity and appeal. Its beloved character evolved because early settlers had extraordinary vision. And though the industries have changed with the times, their legacy has endured and San Diego still attracts visionary men and women. Their input, nurture, and support continue to enhance the quality of life in every sector. As those who live here discovered long ago, one visit is not enough, and the second could last a lifetime.

Pages i–1: Competitive spirit is in the wind, exemplified by this shot of a 1986 MORC (Midget Ocean Racing Club) International Sailboat Race.

San Diego
Cultural History

IT IS ESTIMATED that the indigenous population of the greater San Diego area was around 20,000 when Spanish explorer Juan Rodriguez Cabrillo sailed into San Diego Bay near Ballast Point in 1542. At that time, the local population was composed of groups known as the Luiseño, Cahuilla, Cupeno, Kumeyaay, and Northern Diegueño.

Cabrillo claimed his discovery for the King of Spain and named it San Miguel in honor of St. Michael, the Archangel. He stayed only a week and then quickly sailed north in pursuit of further riches. It was not until Spanish surveyor Sebastian Vizcaino returned in 1602 that San Miguel became San Diego de Alcalá in honor of St. Diego of Alcalá, Spain. Vizcaino, who remained only ten days, found that Cabrillo's maps and written accounts were largely inaccurate as to longitude and latitude, so against strict orders, he renamed everything.

Actual settlement didn't begin for another 160 years, when Spain sent the *San Antonio* to San Diego. The San Carlos soon followed, having become lost due to Vizcaino's faulty directions (Cabrillo wasn't the only one to err), and two parties came overland from Mexico. In the second overland group was Father Junipero Serra, who was charged by Spain to establish missions to the north of San Diego.

Father Serra established the first of 21 missions, Mission San Diego de Alcala, at Presidio Hill in 1769. On the Presidio today there is a magnificent park and the Serra Museum, which is operated by the San Diego Historical Society. Due to the lack of arable land on the Presidio, the original mission was eventually moved six miles east to what is now known as Mission Valley. Open to the public, Mission San Diego de Alcala is still an active parish church.

Opposite: A beautiful señorita dressed in her traditional fiesta costume dances at Old Town's Bazaar del Mundo. *Above:* Junipero Serra Museum on Presidio Hill was named for Father Serra, who founded Mission San Diego de Alcalá, the first of 21 California missions. *Right:* The statue of Juan Rodriguez Cabrillo stands gracefully over the scene at Cabrillo National Monument. *Pages 4-5:* The bells at Mission San Diego de Alcalá are rung in unison once a year on the anniversary of the Mission's founding.

Below the Presidio is Old Town (now a state park), where settlers such as Rafaela Serrano, Pio Pico, Jose Antonio Estudillo, and Juan Bandini built their homes around a central plaza circa 1820-1830. Casa de Bandini is now a restaurant resplendent with hospitable charm and amazing salsa. The twice-restored Casa de Estudillo, which dates from 1827, is said by romantics to be the marriage place of Ramona, the heroine of Helen Hunt Jackson's novel *Ramona*. The casa is open to the public, as are other historic Old Town buildings, including Seeley Stables and San Diego's first newspaper office. San Diego Avenue and Juan Street are lined with historic sites, interesting shops, and wonderful restaurants that offer a variety of cuisine in a range of prices. One can purchase everything from fine art to pottery to postcards.

Extremely popular with tourists, Old Town's Bazaar del Mundo features sixteen international shops, five restaurants, and daily entertainment. In the early 1970s, designer Diane Powers developed the bazaar by transforming the abandoned Casa de Pico Motel (1937), which was originally designed by renowned architect Richard Requa, the director of architecture and landscaping for the 1935 California Pacific International Exposition in Balboa Park.

Moved from other San Diego locations to save them from demolition, seven historic buildings occupy Old Town's Heritage Park (est. 1971). Used for a variety of purposes, the buildings include an 1889 Queen Anne, now a bed and breakfast, and Temple Beth Israel, San Diego's first synagogue.

Above: By day or night, the exterior of the Mormon Temple in La Jolla is a dramatic sight enhanced by the play of light on its surface. This temple was dedicated in 1993, but the historic presence of the Mormons in San Diego dates as far back as 1847. *Below:* These wondrous blossoms sold at Bazaar del Mundo are made of paper. They will last for years without fading.

All Aboard!

An original 1889 Rapid Transit car in a San Diego parade on July 16, 1911.

Today's renowned San Diego Trolley.

Like many other cities, San Diego has had a long love affair with trolleys. In 1886, Elisha S. Babcock Jr. and Hampton L. Story, who built the Hotel Del Coronado, established San Diego's first public transit system. The downtown streetcars, which ran from 5th and L to Broadway and then down to the bay, were drawn by horses and mules and proved such a boon that more lines were soon established.

Competition arrived a year later in the form of electric cars. Then, in the early 1890s, there was a double-deck cable car line that ran from downtown to Park Boulevard. The once dependable mules and horses were out of a job

by 1896. That same year, John D. Spreckels bought the majority of San Diego's Trolley lines, and converted the remaining animal-drawn cars to electricity. In doing so, he created one, uniform streetcar system.

As in cities all over the nation, buses began to replace trolleys in the 1920s and with increasing numbers of automobile owners, trolleys disappeared entirely from San Diego streets by mid-century.

In 1981, the Metropolitan Transit Development Board instituted a fixed-rail transit system called the San Diego Trolley. Over the years since the bright red cars started rolling, San Diego has fallen in love all over again with this historic enterprise.

With its easily identified and beloved bright red cars, the San Diego Trolley serves downtown San Diego with links to Old Town, Qualcomm Stadium, Mission San Diego, the Convention Center, South Bay, the international border at San Ysidro, and East County. In the future, extensions will be added with stops at the University of California at San Diego, located north in La Jolla, and San Diego State University on the east.

Nearby on Twiggs St. is the Theatre in Old Town (1970), a comfy, 250-seat theatre that resembles a barn from the outside. Musical comedy is the usual fare. Next to the theatre is the first stop on the Historic Tours of America Old Town Trolley, which was established in 1989. The trolley takes riders to the Embarcadero, Seaport Village, the downtown Marina, the Convention Center, Horton Plaza, the Gaslamp Quarter, Coronado Island, the San Diego Zoo, and Balboa Park. This narrated tour is a great way for first time visitors to see the city's

highlights without concern for location and logistics. Once a ticket is purchased, trolley riders may, with certain restrictions, jump on and off all day.

Just west of the Trolley stop, Historic Tours is rebuilding the 1853 Casa de Aguirre, which was demolished in 1914. Behind it is a convent, built downtown in 1908 and moved to Old Town in 1940. It has been the first location of the University of San Diego, a seminary building, military housing, a USO dance hall, and housing for several orders of nuns before becoming

Above and Below: A study in contrasts—the modern city juxtaposed with a historic view of San Diego Harbor taken from the Hawthorne Inn, circa 1900.

Camp Pendleton

Camp Pendleton was built on Mexican grant land known as Rancho Santa Margarita y Las Flores, originally owned by the last Mexican governor of California, Pio Pico, and his brother Andres. Starting at 125,000 acres, Camp Pendleton was established as the largest Marine Corps base on the West Coast. It was named for Major General Joseph H. Pendleton, who pioneered Marine activities in the greater San Diego area. Built in only five months, Camp Pendleton was officially dedicated by President Franklin Delano Roosevelt in September 1942.

The base was tremendously important as a training and replacement command during WWII, and during the Korean War alone, 200,000 Marines passed through on their way to the Far East. More recently, Camp Pendleton was able to deploy troops and equipment halfway around the world in a matter of days for Desert Storm and Desert Shield. Its capability to do so continues with present deployments in the Middle East.

Its terrain, including seventeen miles of shoreline, allows an array of inland, airborne, and amphibious training sites. There are firing, bombing, and strafing ranges; parachute drop zones; three mock urban warfare sites; and areas for large-scale tactical maneuvers.

Tours of base museums and the original Ranch House, bunkhouse, and chapel can be scheduled Tuesdays and Thursdays at 10 a.m. from late September to the end of May and must be applied for in writing to CPAO H&S Bn, Attn: History and Museums Office, Marine Corps Base, Box 555019, Camp Pendleton, CA 92055-5019.

derelict. Both Casa de Aguirre and the convent are scheduled to reopen in the spring of 2003. They will contain shops, offices, food service, and an exhibition of artifacts from the 1850s recovered during recent archaeological digs.

The Old Town Trolley also celebrates San Diego's rich military history with its "Tour of Patriotism" offered on Tuesdays. For those not familiar with the city's early military relationships, this tour is a must.

The first U.S. warship to enter the San Diego harbor was the *Cyane* on July 29, 1846. Marine and Navy personnel came ashore, raised the flag in Old Town and established Ft. Stockton on the Presidio. In 1910, the Marines were billeted at North Island. During the California Pacific Exposition, they maintained barracks and a model Marine camp in Balboa Park and then finally moved to Dutch Flats in 1921.

In 1927, a few years after the Marines took up residence at Dutch Flats, Ryan Aircraft built Charles A. Lindbergh's *Spirit of St. Louis*. In honor of this historic flight from New York to Paris, San Diego's airport is named Lindbergh Field. Aeronautical buffs will find fighter plane history and displays at USMC Air Station Miramar, and in Balboa Park at the Aerospace Museum and the Reuben H. Fleet Space and Science Center.

The mutually beneficial relationship established between California and the U.S. military proudly continues to this day. Present-day military bases and installations include Naval Air Station North Island, Naval Amphibious Base Coronado, Marine Corps. Air Station, Miramar, the Marine Corps. Base Camp Pendleton in Oceanside, and the U.S. Coast Guard located on the Embarcadero near Lindbergh Field.

Above and Below: The glorious sight of docked Naval ships awaiting provisions is common in San Diego.

San Diego
Entertainment

TODAY, DOWNTOWN SAN DIEGO and the adjacent Gaslamp Quarter are alive with people, all seeking amusement. Whether it is a gourmet dining experience, a night of cool jazz, or a visit with entertainment in San Diego are guaranteed success. Surprisingly, this was not always the case.

Like so many across the nation, San Diego's downtown began to lose its luster after World War II, when the population began moving into the suburbs, inevitably causing the merchants to follow. The major department stores closed or moved to outlying malls. Even San Diego's major newspapers forsook downtown and moved to Mission Valley. The once bustling downtown found itself rife with vacant buildings.

In 1974, merchants and property owners formed the Gaslamp Quarter Association, and the year following, the City of San Diego instituted the non-profit Centre City Development Corporation to assist on redevelopment efforts by cultivating retail, residential, office, hotel, cultural, and educational projects. More than a quarter century later it can be said that success crowned these efforts.

Horton Plaza, anchored by several major department stores that were enticed back downtown, was definitely a catalyst. It is a multi-level shopping center designed by architect Jon Jerde and built in 1985 by developer Ernest Hahn. Jerde described the diagonally laid out mall as "an abstraction of indigenous architectural language…reflecting San Diego's rich history."

Opposite: Painted 23 different colors, Horton Plaza was crucial in the development of San Diego's Gaslamp Quarter. The 22-foot high Jessop's clock in the foreground was built in 1907 and would cost $2 million to replace. *Above:* The landmark lights in today's Gaslamp Quarter are not actual gas lamps, but they do catch the eye. *Top:* Caribbean Flamingos, part of a spectacular flock, delight San Diego Zoo visitors. Their pink color is dependent upon a diet of shrimp. *Right:* Sailboats rest on the sand at 4,000-acre Mission Bay Park, the West Coast's largest aquatic park.

At the base of artist Joan Brown's "Obelisk" in Horton Plaza is the two-theatre complex known as the Lyceum, administered and utilized by the San Diego Repertory Theatre, known to all as "the Rep." Rep productions range from musicals and plays, to an annual production of Charles Dickens' *A Christmas Carol*. In a unique arrangement with the city, the Rep extends management services and co-production arrangements to other San Diego performing arts groups and community organizations on a year-round basis. Artistic Director Sam

Woodhouse thinks of his downtown theatre as a cultural town hall where people of all kinds can come together to achieve greater understanding through the arts.

Adjacent to Horton Plaza, in what is called Horton Square, artist Jesus Dominguez' statue of Alonzo Horton shows the city father proudly holding a map of his original 800-acre downtown purchase, for which he paid $265. If he could see San Diego now, he would wear an even broader smile.

The Gaslamp Quarter, which is the historic core of downtown, now burgeons with residential properties, hotels, new office buildings, and a nightclub scene that caused it to be termed "the New Orleans of the West." Overall, it covers sixteen-and-a-half square blocks and eventually becomes the gateway to the bay front Embarcadero and the San Diego Convention Center. The Convention Center, proclaimed one of the loveliest in the world, opened in 1989, and was expanded in 2001. And just across the street is a treasure that must be experienced on foot. It is the Martin Luther King Jr. Promenade, a half-mile path in a park that runs parallel to Harbor Drive. Markers along the route bear inspirational quotes from the civil rights leader, including an excerpt from his "I Have a Dream" speech.

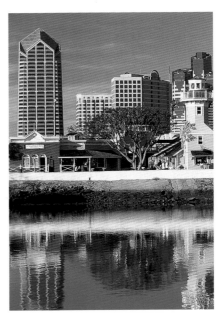

Top: The San Diego Convention Center boasts more than one million square feet and one display room larger than a football field. *Above:* Seaport Village as seen from San Diego Bay. *Left:* Downtown San Diego as seen from Harbor Island, one of two man-made islands in the bay. *Opposite:* Located on Shelter Island, this is only one of San Diego's first-class marinas. *Pages 14-15:* The famous *Star of India*, an attraction of the Maritime Museum on the Embarcadero.

Who is that Ancient Mariner?

For all those sea savvy visitors, a trip to the Maritime Museum is definitely in order. The major attractions in the museum's fleet are the world's oldest, active sailing ship, *Star of India*, and *Berkeley*, both open daily.

An iron ship, *Star of India* was christened *Euterpe* and was built at the Isle of Man in 1863. She circumnavigated the globe twenty-one times while transporting emigrants from Ireland, England, and Scotland to New Zealand, and also made ports of call in Australia, Chile, and California. Renamed *Star of India* under new ownership in 1906, the ship became passé in an era of steamships. In 1926, she was purchased by a group of San Diegans and, after falling into disrepair, was fully restored. Alongside *Star of India*, visitors find the steam-powered ferryboat *Berkeley* (1898), whose main claim to fame was saving the lives of survivors fleeing the fire that followed the 1906 San Francisco earthquake.

Because these ships have such a colorful past, it comes as no surprise that they are said to be haunted. In the late 1970s, a Maritime Museum employee reported seeing a ghostly form walking across the deck of the *Berkley* through a thick fog. As the employee approached the apparition, it suddenly disappeared (John J. Lamb, *San Diego Specters*, Sunbelt Publications).

Star of India is widely reputed to have two ghosts, one a Scotsman stowaway named John Campbell, who fell from the mast and died after three days of excruciating pain, and the other a Chinese seaman, who was crushed to death by the ship's anchor chains. It is now said that these ghosts are doomed to sail the seas for eternity.

There haven't been any recent sightings reported, but visitors to San Diego's haunted ships claim that they feel a chill in the air as they pass by dark shadows. But don't let the ghosts keep you away, a visit to the Maritime Museum is highly entertaining whether you have a ghostly encounter or not.

Just north of the Convention Center is Seaport Village, a quaint, waterfront shopping mall. Numerous restaurants overlook a beautiful marina and park. Though not historic, Seaport Village is home to the Broadway Flying Horses Carousel, built at New York's Coney Island in 1890. Children of all ages may ride while listening to a German-built pipe organ that dates from 1914.

Beginning at the Seaport Village boardwalk you may amble as far north as Harbor Island. Along the way is the Cruise Terminal, which accommodated 120 cruise ships in 2002, eighty of them beginning or ending a voyage in San Diego. The Cruise Terminal offers stunning views of downtown and its beautiful skyline.

Also nearby is the renowned Anthony's Fish Grotto and Star of the Sea Room. Just north are the San Diego Maritime Museum and the Coast Guard Station. Harbor Island, which offers spectacular views of the city, is really a man-made peninsula dotted with hotels and restaurants. It also features a public park, walking trail, boat ramp, and fishing pier.

Top: A tranquil spot for repose in the midst of Seaport Village.
Left: Seaport Village's beautifully landscaped grounds.
Bottom: The Broadway Flying Horses Carousel at Seaport Village is a child's paradise.
Pages 18-19: The Embarcadero at dusk.

Dining Delights

There are countless places to "grab a bite" in San Diego, but if you want something out of the ordinary, the following suggestions should lead you in the right direction.

Fun family restaurants abound in the greater San Diego area, but highly recommended is the local chain known as Sammy's Wood-fired Pizza, where the salads, pasta, and pizza are always served fresh and to your order. Another favorite is Mazara's in North Park with its authentic home-cooked Italian meals. They also offer family specials, which are posted nightly. The Old Spaghetti Factory in the Gaslamp Quarter is a sure-fire hit for everyone, and at Crest Café in Hillcrest, you'll find the best burgers and fries outside of your own kitchen.

For those looking for a more sophisticated dining experience, The Prado Restaurant in Balboa Park's House of Hospitality offers fabulous outdoor seating in a Moorish garden, which may be preceded by appetizers and drinks in a cozy lounge. Albert's at the San Diego Zoo not only serves up the gourmet experience, but you will feel as if you're on an African safari in this elegant, treetop restaurant. Speaking of animals, try Rhinoceros in Coronado for an excellent dinner selection, among which the favorites are New York steak, thick cut pork chops, and a variety of pasta dishes.

While in Hillcrest, visit the local favorites Arrivederci or Bai Yook. At Arrivederci you will find friendly service, traditionally prepared Italian entrees, an amazing seafood pasta, fine wines, and unbeatable tiramisu. And you will not find better Thai food than at Bai Yook, nestled in the corner of a strip mall on University Avenue. Finally, it is worth the drive to North Park to dine at Tioli's, where the experience is truly unique. The chef and owner, Willie Pelletier, travels the world for inspiration, a fact to which his ever-changing creations attest.

If you are craving Mexican food, look no farther than Bazaar Del Mundo's Casa Bandini or Casa de Pico. Both restaurants will welcome you with Mexican hospitality and the best authentic food this side of the border. For a Californian twist on the old Mexican favorites, Chuey's near Coronado Bridge is highly recommended.

And because you're on the coast, you'll want fresh seafood. King's Fish House in Mission Valley always has the best of the local catch. Also good are Peohe's at the Ferry Landing in Coronado and Sally's on the waterfront in the Hyatt Hotel at Seaport Village. You won't be able to beat the views or the high quality food. No matter what your tastes are, San Diego dining has something for everyone.

Casa de Pico in Old Town's Bazaar del Mundo.

Olé Madrid, one of the Gaslamp Quarter's many cafés.

Casa Bandini, a Mexican food favorite.

Located in Mission Valley just northeast of downtown is Qualcomm Stadium, a multi-purpose sports facility originally built at a cost of $27.5 million in 1967. With a seating capacity of 71,500, the stadium accommodates major league baseball and football teams, concerts, and off-road events. It hosted the Major League World Series in 1984 and 1998, the Major League Baseball All-Star Game in 1978 and 1992, and the Super Bowl in 1988, 1998, and 2003. Sports records achieved there include Willie Mays' 600th home run on September 22, 1969 and Lou Brock's 892nd stolen base on August 29, 1977. Memorable concerts include the Rolling Stones, The

Who, U2, Pink Floyd, and Elton John and Billy Joel.

Until 1980 the Stadium was simply known as San Diego Stadium, and then it was named for sports writer Jack Murphy, who was instrumental in persuading the city to build it. The stadium was renamed Qualcomm in 1997 in return for money to fund an expansion project. Currently, the San Diego Padres, tenants since 1969, await completion of San Diego's new baseball stadium in East Village (just east of downtown), which is scheduled for completion in 2004. The new ballpark complex is within walking distance of the trolley, the waterfront, the Convention Center, and many downtown hotels and restaurants.

Below: The San Diego Padres host the Arizona Diamondbacks at Qualcomm Stadium.
Opposite: A tranquil sail at sunset.

San Diego's Seaside Celebrity

Did you know that SeaWorld's famous killer whale, Shamu, eats 250 pounds of fish every day? Or that adult manatees weigh between 800 and 1,200 pounds and are vegetarians? They eat huge water hyacinths, which are hard on the teeth, so nature made them extremely adaptable. When their teeth wear out, new ones grow in to replace them!

These are just a few of the fascinating educational facts observant families learn at SeaWorld, which since its opening in 1964 has attracted more than 100 million guests. On more than one hundred gorgeous acres located in Mission Bay Park, visitors delight in one of the world's largest amusement parks. Among the amusements is the park's newest ride, Shipwreck Rapids, which simulates a wild raft trip down a raging river. SeaWorld's landmark tower rises 325 feet. Riding to the top is very popular and you get a bird's eye view of San Diego. Another neat attraction is Wild Arctic, where you can get a close up view of a polar bear and take a simulated helicopter ride to an arctic station.

The animals are the main attraction, though, and you will see sea lions, otters, those immense manatees, the aforementioned Shamu and kin, and six species of the tuxedo-clad penguins. You may also feed the dolphins, that is, if you don't mind the smell of fish. What most people like the best are the human and animal interactive shows in various lagoons. But watch out—Shamu might just get you all wet!

Killer Whale Show

Emperor Penguin

DID YOU KNOW...

■ **THE BLUE WHALE** is the largest animal in the world, and its heart alone can weigh 2,000 pounds.

■ **A BULLFROG** has teeth in the roof of its mouth and will eat almost anything that moves, even other frogs.

■ **GREEN SEA TURTLES** can stay underwater as long as five hours. To conserve oxygen, their hearts slow to one beat every nine minutes.

■ **THE IBIS** was worshipped in ancient Egyptian societies as the god Thoth. The birds were so sacred that they were often mummified and buried with pharaohs.

■ **MARABOU STORKS** are attracted to grass fires. They march in front of the advancing fire and prey on animals that are fleeing.

■ **BABY HIPPOS** can swim the moment they are born, because they are born underwater.

■ **THE BLUE SEA STAR** can regenerate an entire new body from the base of a single severed arm.

■ **POLAR BEARS** are among the largest land carnivores, weighing as much as 1,433 pounds, and have been known to swim continuously for 62 miles.

■ **A FLAMINGO'S** ankle is located halfway up its leg, and its knee is located close to the body and is not externally visible.

■ **BOTTLENOSE DOLPHINS** often cooperate when hungry by encircling a school of fish and herding them into a tight ball. Then they take turns charging through the school to feed.

Reprinted courtesy of SeaWorld, San Diego

Killer Whale

Polar Bear and admirer

San Diego's oldest and perhaps greatest fun family attraction is the San Diego Zoo, located north of downtown on Park Boulevard. The Zoological Society was founded in 1916 by Dr. Harry Wegeforth, who was concerned about the fate of animals displayed at the 1915-1916 Panama-California Exposition. A Midwesterner by birth and a lifelong lover of animals, Wegeforth enjoyed a thriving medical practice long before he became a zealous advocate for the San Diego Zoo.

Today's zoo, which occupies one hundred acres, is acknowledged by many to be one of the finest in the world. It hosts and nurtures 4,000 individual animals that represent 800 different species. Additionally, the plant population exceeds 6,500 species and is one of the most extensive botanical collections in existence.

Zoo terrain is hilly and first-time visitors may want to get acquainted via the forty-minute guided bus tour that covers about seventy- five percent of the exhibit areas. Tour bus riders also have access to the express bus, which stops at five different locations to unload guests who may want to hop off for more leisurely explorations. Riders may get on and off the bus at designated stops anytime they wish.

Opposite: **Sumatra Orangutan.** *Left (Top to Bottom):* **Tiger, Lemur, Green Tree Python, Polar Bear, Transvaal Lion.** *Above:* **Playful African River Hippos.** *Right:* **A watchful Gazelle.**

Children of all ages have long enjoyed the antics of sea lions at Wegeforth Bowl's Sea Lion Show. The Wild Ones, which takes place at Hunte Amphitheatre, demonstrates the behaviors of wild predators and their prey. Each of these free shows is offered several times a day.

Exhibits not to be missed are Tiger River, Polar Bear Plunge, Gorilla Tropics, Scripps Aviary, the Bonobos (chimpanzee cousins), and Sun Bear Forest. All animals are displayed in habitats that approximate their natural state in the wild.

While in San Diego you will also want to spend a day in lovely, historic Coronado, which offers a variety of entertainment, including shopping, theatre, and bayside sightseeing. To get there, take the Coronado Bridge, certainly one of the most beautiful spans ever created. It was completed in 1969 to connect San Diego to North Island Naval Air Station and Coronado.

Beneath the bridge on the San Diego side is a unique city park that surrounds the largest collection of Chicano murals in the world. Called "the architect of the dream," resident and artist Salvador Roberto Torres envisioned murals on the bridge supports. After traveling to Mexico to study the works of muralists Jose Luis Orozco, David Alfaro Siquieros, and Diego Rivera, Torres began working on the murals in 1973. The resulting spectacle has attracted worldwide attention.

Though some still call it Coronado *Island*, that is a misnomer. Coronado is really a thirteen-and-a-half square-mile peninsula. Located at the south end is the Hotel del Coronado.

Top Left: The serene face of a Sea Lion.
Top Right: Sunset provides a picturesque backdrop for the Coronado Bridge.
Left: A small sample of the world-famous Chicano Park murals. *Opposite:* A visit to the Point Loma Lighthouse offers wonderful views of the ocean and insight into San Diego's colorful history.

San Diego's Guiding Light

When California became a state in 1850, the need for
a lighthouse became pressing. It was constructed in
1855 at what seemed to be a good site 422 feet above
sea level between the bay and the ocean, not too far
from Juan Rodriguez Cabrillo's original landing spot
at Ballast Point. The site proved problematic, however,
because prevailing climatic conditions—low lying clouds
and constant fog—made seeing the light difficult if
not impossible.

In 1891, the old lighthouse was closed and a new
lighthouse was built one hundred yards south, which
was much closer to the water. The old lighthouse,
restored in 1935, is now the jewel of the 160-acre
Cabrillo National Monument, which typically receives
more than 1,000,000 visitors annually. Views of the
ocean and the bay are spectacular, and the visitor center
offers a bookstore, ranger-led discovery programs, and
an exhibit entitled "The Age of Exploration." Visitors
can learn more about Cabrillo, the discoverer of San
Diego, whose heroic limestone statue by Portuguese
artist Charters de Almeida presides majestically over
the point. This attraction is not to be missed.

Point Loma Lighthouse

The Hotel Del, as locals affectionately call it, is Coronado's undisputed crown jewel. Completed in 1888, it has hosted presidents, kings, and Hollywood moguls such as Marilyn Monroe and Tony Curtis, who filmed *Some Like It Hot* at the hotel in 1958.

Designed by James and Watson Reid, Hotel Del was initially owned by Elijah S. Babcock and Hampton L. Story. Babcock became indebted to sugar heir John D. Spreckels and sold the hotel to him in 1900. Spreckels set about making improvements and put up tents south of the hotel to accommodate summer guests. Tent City, as it was called, proved so popular that it endured until 1939.

Orange Avenue offers additional diversions, including Bay Books, one of San Diego's most inviting independent bookstores, and Café 1134, a truly wonderful coffee shop next to Lamb's Players Theatre. Lamb's Players Theatre is one of San Diego's most popular theatres and the third largest in terms of budget. Lamb's is located in a renovated neoclassical structure originally designed by Harrison Albright for John D. Spreckels, who wanted Coronado to have a theatre. When completed in 1917, the property housed a bank, twelve shops, eleven

Some Like It Hot

apartments, and the theatre, inaugurated by Mme. Ernestine Schumann-Heink, a famous singer of the day. Among the celebrities who graced its stage was conductor/composer John Philip Sousa. Albright also designed Spreckels' Coronado mansion (now the Glorietta Bay Inn), Balboa Park's Organ Pavilion, and the ornate, still utilized 1,915-seat Spreckels Theatre, located in downtown San Diego.

Above Left: The historic Hotel del Coronado.
Above Right: Tony Curtis, Jack Lemmon, and Marilyn Monroe in *Some Like It Hot*, which was filmed at the Hotel del Coronado in 1958.
Below: Extra rooms were provided for summer guests in Tent City outside of Hotel del Coronado, circa 1904.

Top: **Ferry Landing Marketplace provides an array of activities, food, and entertainment.**
Above: **Visitors to Coronado will be taken in by the charming façades on Orange Avenue.**
Pages 30-31: **Windsurfers take advantage of a beautiful day.**

At the north end of Coronado is the Ferry Landing Marketplace with shops, restaurants, a spectacular view of San Diego, and a passenger ferry to the Embarcadero. There are miles of biking, skating, and walking paths on Coronado, plus eighteen tennis courts and a championship golf course.

But San Diego is much more than the Gaslamp Quarter, downtown, and Coronado. It abounds with quaint neighborhoods, beloved of residents, and less often seen by the casual visitor. Each is unique in flavor and appeal. Among the most interesting are Little Italy, Hillcrest, Ocean Beach, Golden Hill, and North and South Park. Neighborhood architecture ranges from the bizarrely colored new condos and apartments of trendy Little Italy, to the fabulously restored Victorian mansions along Granada Avenue in South Park, to a kaleido-scope of well-maintained California Craftsman cottages in North Park.

Among the more fascinating and off-the-beaten path things to do outside of the city center is to tour the fabulously restored Victorian home called the "Painted Lady" and to investigate the past of its notorious first owner, Jesse Shepard. Open Friday through Sunday, the Villa is maintained by the San Diego Historical Society and furnished with period antiques, some originally owned by Shepard.

Another area of interest is Ocean Beach, where you will still find remnants of the flower child culture of the 1960s. On the busy streets by the Ocean Beach Pier, you will find tie-dye clothing shops, antique stores, an organic food market, and coffee shops with impromptu poetry readings.

It is possible to take the boardwalk from the Ocean Beach Pier to Pacific Beach, en route passing Belmont Park and stopping for a ride on the restored 1925 Giant Dipper roller coaster, in service every day. You will also pass through Mission Beach, which settled itself along a strip where the Pacific Ocean and Mission Bay are only blocks apart. The boardwalk is an ever-changing kaleidoscope of activity. On the bay side are well-tended waterfront homes and quiet harbors, and on the ocean side are long stretches of white sand washed by spectacular waves. Soon after passing Pacific Beach's historic Crystal Pier, with its stretch of white cottages, comes the end of the coast walk.

La Jolla, which has a unique atmosphere, lies just north of Pacific Beach. It is one of the most beautiful and relatively unspoiled beach towns in the U.S. There's diving and snorkeling in the Cove and Harbor seals at the Children's Pool.

Farther north at La Jolla Shores is a fine, sandy beach. The Village is the thing, though, when in La Jolla. Residents still call the main shopping area "The Village." It is known for its shops, art galleries, restaurants, and the Museum of Contemporary Art, which embraces the Irving Gill-designed home once owned by Scripps Newspapers heiress Ellen Browning Scripps. Scripps' beneficiaries include the Scripps Institution of Oceanography, Scripps Hospital and Clinic, the Gill-designed La Jolla Women's Club, the Children's Pool at La Jolla Cove, and the La Jolla Recreation Center, also designed by Gill.

Left: Lines for the Giant Dipper Roller Coaster grow on the opening day of Belmont Amusement Park in Mission Beach, July 4, 1925.
Below: An aerial view of Seal Rock Reserve, the Children's Pool, and the Museum of Contemporary Art, La Jolla. *Bottom:* Pacific Beach's historic Crystal Pier at sunset.
Opposite: Harbor seals are often found sunning at the Children's Pool in La Jolla.
Pages 34-35: Enormous sand sculptures such as this one called "Atlantis," supervised by Gerry Kirk, are created for competitions each year.

Along Girard Avenue, La Jolla boasts several independent bookstores worth investigating, including D.G. Wills Book Store and Warwick's. Also fabulous is John Cole's Books near the Museum of Contemporary Art.

A bit farther north, the University of California, San Diego (founded in 1960), is worth exploring for its outdoor art and architectural wonders, which include the Stuart Collection of sculpture and the much-photographed Geisel Library, designed by William L. Pereira Associates. Also on campus is the Tony Award-winning La Jolla Playhouse, which presents classics, new plays and musicals, and is the birthplace of such Broadway fare as *Big River*, *The Who's Tommy*, and *Thoroughly Modern Millie*. The Playhouse was founded in 1947 by film and stage stars Gregory Peck, Dorothy McGuire, and Mel Ferrer and was revived at its current location in 1983.

The Stephen Birch Aquarium at Scripps Institution of Oceanography has more than thirty tanks and an outdoor, hands-on tide pool. In addition to exotic tropical fish, you will find sea horses, anemones, and specimens from local waters including the Garibaldi, leopard sharks, sea bass, whitefish, and tuna.

Opposite: Surfers catch the last wave at sunset. *Top:* A vibrant red starfish in the tide pool at the Stephen Birch Aquarium at Scripps Institution of Oceanography. *Middle:* Visitors peer into one of the immense fish tanks at Birch Aquarium. *Bottom:* Tropical species inhabit the smaller tanks at Birch Aquarium.

Historic La Jolla was settled by those wanting a picturesque weekend getaway from the hustle and bustle of turn-of-the-century San Diego, a four-hour trek in those days. The Green Dragon artist colony was built on a rise overlooking the ocean in 1894. Adapted for commercial use, remnants of the colony are still visible. Dating from 1894, Brockton Villa occupies property that Dr. Joseph Rodes purchased for $165. Now a popular restaurant, it offers a wealth of fascinating history and spectacular views of the La Jolla coastline.

Visitors who love the outdoors are urged to visit the 1,000-acre Torrey Pines State Reserve, which preserves native flora and fauna, including the beautiful and rare Torrey Pines. There are spectacular views from the reserve's peaceful eight-mile walking trail (pack your own water), and a lagoon frequented by migrating sea birds, including 235 species at last count. Weekend guided walks begin at the visitor center, commissioned in 1922 by Ellen Browning Scripps.

No matter what your interests are, a visit to San Diego can be a most satisfying experience. Whether it's whale watching at Sea World, attending a classic production of *A Christmas Carol* at the Rep., shopping in "the Village," or taking long meandering hikes through Torrey Pines State Reserve, San Diego's got it all.

Opposite: Parasailing is a popular sport at Torrey Pines Gliderport, open since 1928. Charles A. Lindbergh set a record in 1930 when he soared from the top of Mt. Soledad, along the Torrey Pines cliffs past the Gliderport, and landed on the beach in Del Mar. *Top:* Designed and built by Billy Bell in the 1950s, Torrey Pines Golf Course offers two 18-hole courses open to the public. Site of the Buick Invitational, the course is one of the world's most beautiful. *Above:* Miles of walking paths are available at Torrey Pines State Reserve for active visitors.

San Diego
Arts & Culture

AS EARLY AS 1868 Alonzo Horton and Ephriam W. Morse recommended to city trustees that 1,400 acres of land be reserved for a city park. Jackrabbits and coyotes abounded on the cactus- and chaparral-laden tract, which the *San Diego Union* pronounced "unfit for any private uses."

Nothing much happened at "City Park" as it was then called, at least for a while, but the city was able to successfully ward off most of those who wanted to bite off a chunk of the land for themselves. An exception was made in the case of horticulturist Kate Sessions. In 1892, she was given a lease on 30 acres of parkland, where she established a nursery. In exchange, she promised to plant 100 trees in the park each year. Ruth Hayward's sculpture of Sessions, dedicated in 1998, welcomes visitors at the park's west entrance.

Sessions propagated seeds gathered from around the world and introduced young trees, shrubs, and vines to San Diego's rich soil. Sessions is responsible for the profusion and variety of plant life seen in San Diego today, including jacaranda, palms, birds of paradise, bougainvillea, Torrey pines, oaks, pepper trees, and eucalyptus.

Today, Balboa Park, which was named for Spanish explorer Vasco Nuñez de Balboa (1475-1519), boasts 15,000 trees that are maintained by the San Diego Park and Recreation Department's dedicated staff of horticultural experts and gardeners. The best known tree is a Moreton Bay Fig planted prior to 1915. Located just north of the Natural History Museum, it is 60 feet tall with a spread of 120 feet.

Opposite: The blue heron sits patiently among the lily pads, looking for his catch of the day at Balboa Park's Lily Pond.
Above: Visitors stroll aross the pedestrian mall in front of the Casa del Prado.
Below: The Bea Evenson fountain in Balboa Park is beautiful at dusk.

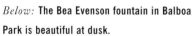

Passport to Balboa Park

The Passport to Balboa Park, available at the House of Hospitality Visitors Center, offers savings on admission to popular park institutions.

- SAN DIEGO MUSEUM of ART
- SAN DIEGO AEROSPACE MUSEUM
- SAN DIEGO AUTOMOTIVE MUSEUM
- MUSEUM of SAN DIEGO HISTORY
- MUSEUM of PHOTOGRAPHIC ARTS
- SAN DIEGO NATURAL HISTORY MUSEUM
- SAN DIEGO HALL of CHAMPIONS SPORTS MUSEUM
- SAN DIEGO MUSEUM of MAN
- SAN DIEGO MODEL RAILROAD MUSEUM
- REUBEN H. FLEET SCIENCE CENTER
- SAN DIEGO ART INSTITUTE
- MINGEI INTERNATIONAL MUSEUM
- JAPANESE FRIENDSHIP GARDEN

Opposite: El Cid, represented in this twenty-three-foot statue, was actually Rodrigo Diaz de Bivar (1040-1099), the hero of Spain's war against the Moors. *Below:* Casa de Balboa on the Prado looking east in 1916.
Pages 44-45: Neatly trimmed hedges in Alcazar Garden allow visitors to take a peaceful midday stroll.

Two expositions shaped the artistic future of Balboa Park. The Panama-California Exposition was held in 1915-1916 to celebrate the opening of the Panama Canal. Even though San Francisco had a similar exposition that year, San Diego's well-planned event put the city on the West Coast cultural map. Twenty years later Balboa Park hosted a second fair, the California Pacific International Exposition. This event was so popular it extended into 1936.

Each exposition left a legacy of Spanish Colonial and Mission Revival buildings. Some were preserved, giving Balboa Park an exotic grandeur and unique architectural charm. Over the years, the historic structures were renovated or, in some cases, torn down and meticulously rebuilt with modern materials to replicate their original design and make them compliant with modern earthquake safety standards.

Built for the 1915 exposition, the House of Hospitality was remodeled by lead architect Richard Requa for the 1935 exposition. First-time park visitors are urged to begin their Balboa Park acquaintanceship at the House of Hospitality Visitors Center. There is a fine gift shop with friendly volunteers and a good selection of guidebooks, maps, and brochures about park institutions, attractions, and special exhibits.

Also available is the Passport to Balboa Park. Good for a week, it affords savings on admission to park institutions. True museum lovers might be able to cover two institutions per day and, depending on the focus and range of their interests, might allot as long as a week to see and savor everything.

Most of the institutions are located along the Prado, a wide pedestrian mall that cuts through the park from west to east. Consider boarding the free red tram, which is actually a bus, at the House of Hospitality. It provides a narrated overview of park attractions.

In front of the House of Hospitality on the Plaza de Panama is one of Balboa Park's most recognizable landmarks, Anna Hyatt Huntington's statue, "El Cid," dedicated in 1930. Astride a stunningly muscled stallion is the heroic El Cid, who according to legend drove the Moors from Valencia.

Located across the Prado from the Visitors Center, the Botanical Building was unveiled in 1915. At the time, it was the largest wood lath construction in the world. In its inviting depths there are around 2,100 "resident" tropicals and seasonal displays as well. One of the most photographed park images is the Botanical Building as seen from the far side of the large Lily Pond, one of two reflecting pools originally called *Las Lagunas de las Flores* (The Lakes of the Flowers). The large pond is planted with exotic aquatic specimens, lilies, and lotus that bloom spectacularly during summer and fall.

When the U.S. Navy took over Balboa Park during World War I, the Lily Pond was used for boat drills and swimming lessons, though such things are difficult to imagine. More recently, the ponds were home to outcast San Diego goldfish, an early morning snack for the great heron that fished from atop the Botanical Building's façade.

The House of Charm, known as the Indian Arts Building in 1915, was rebuilt from the ground up and reopened in 1996. Its four levels embrace three organizations: the Mingei International Museum, which faces on the Plaza de Panama, the San Diego Art Institute, which is entered from the Prado, and the underground rehearsal facilities of the Globe Theatres.

Behind the House of Charm is Alcazar Garden, designed in 1935 by Richard Requa and inspired by a castle garden in Seville. Here visitors find colorful annual plantings in formal beds surrounded by hedges. The garden has two star-shaped fountains with multi-colored Moorish tiles. Other features include a pergola and numerous tile and stone benches from which to gaze upon the flowers.

Established in 1974, The Mingei International Museum is dedicated to fostering world understanding through the arts of the people. Some exhibits are drawn from the museum's vast

permanent collection; others are special exhibits from around the world. All are colorful, vibrant and beautifully displayed. Not to be missed in the rotunda is Niki de Saint Phalle's "Angel of Temperance." Outside the entrance are two permanent installations by the late, great Saint Phalle: "Poets and Muses" and the "Niki-gator" a great favorite with children, who play in and on the work.

Dedicated to the promotion of San Diego County's emerging artists, the Art Institute annually presents more than thirty exhibitions in its 10,000 square-foot facility, accessed from the Prado. There is an excellent gift shop featuring unique artist creations, such as hand-painted scarves and stoles.

The Old Globe Theatre, now known as The Globe Theatres, was built in 1935 as an attraction of the California Pacific International Exposition. Billed as a replica of Shakespeare's London Globe Theatre, it was occupied by a troupe of young professionals who enacted fifty-minute versions of Shakespeare's plays before enthralled fairgoers. At the close of the fair, the temporary buildings were slated for the wrecking ball, but arts-minded citizens raised funds for renovation and established a not-for-profit corporation that endures to the present. Annually, the Tony Award-winning Globe presents thirteen

Top: This view of the Botanical Building as seen from the far side of the lily pond is one of the most photographed places in Balboa Park. *Above:* The Old Globe Theatre was built in 1935 as a replica of Shakespeare's London Globe Theatre. *Opposite Top:* The façade of the San Diego Museum of Art features statues of Spanish artists Diego Velasquez, Bartolomé Esteban Murillo, and Francisco de Zurbaran. *Opposite Bottom:* The spacious John M. and Sally B. Thornton Rotunda, San Diego Museum of Art.

productions and is a breeding ground for Broadway-bound works. Backstage tours are available Saturday and Sunday mornings.

Next to the Globe complex is Balboa Park's landmark California Building, designed by Bertram Goodhue for the 1915 fair. The ornate building features a carillon tower and tiled rotunda and houses the anthropological exhibitions of the San Diego Museum of Man. The museum places emphasis on the native cultures of the Western Americas, but it has also been known to display an Egyptian mummy or two.

Proceeding east along the Prado is the San Diego Museum of Art, a later addition to the park designed by William Templeton Johnson and opened in 1926. The San Diego Museum of Art boasts a fine sculpture garden and an outstanding collection of European, Asian, and American art. The museum hosts touring exhibitions of high quality. Free tours are offered with admission Tuesday through Sunday.

Opposite: An impressive collection of Morpho butterflies, Museum of Natural History.
Above: A graceful whale sculpture greets guests at the Museum of Natural History.
Below: The colorful entrance to Centro Cultural de la Raza. *Pages 50-51:* The whale exhibit in the Natural History Museum is replete with an entire whale jaw.

Admission is always free at the adjacent Timken Museum of Art, a modern building opened in 1965 to house the Putnam Collection, amassed by two unmarried sisters who were heirs to the Timken Roller Bearing fortune. The art spans six centuries and includes works by Rembrandt, Breugel the Elder, and Reubens, plus the work of 19th century European and American artists.

Across from the Botanical Building the rebuilt Casa de Balboa embraces the Museum of Photographic Arts, the San Diego Historical Society Museum and archives, and the San Diego Model Railroad Museum. The Museum of Photographic Arts, which enjoys a national reputation for excellence, sometimes originates traveling exhibitions. The Historical Society Museum presents changing and permanent exhibitions that investigate San Diego's history from the 1840s onward. Its one hundred-seat Thornton Theatre is the home of the San Diego Cinema Society. Finally, a great favorite with children of all ages, the San Diego Model Railroad Museum features exhibitions of the Cabrillo & Southwestern, San Diego & Arizona Eastern, Tehachapi Pass, and Pacific Desert Lines, plus a toy train gallery. Watching the scale models whiz through miniature landscapes is great family fun.

The Prado ends at the east side of Balboa Park in a plaza flanked by the San Diego Natural History Museum and the Reuben H. Fleet Science Center. In this plaza is the beautiful Bea Evenson Memorial Fountain, which shoots water sixty feet into the air. Beautiful by day or by night, its wide, tiled lip invites one to sit and relax in the architectural grandeur of the park.

Designed by William Templeton Johnson, the Natural History Museum was opened in 1933, and thereby hangs a tale. Left over from the 1915 exposition, the imposing Southern California Counties Building, later known as the Civic Auditorium, stood on this spot until it burned down in 1925. Oddly enough, the Fireman's Ball was to be held there that very night. Needless to say, no dancing was done. The Counties Building was razed and the Natural History Museum took its place. The museum features minerals, animals, and plants native to the San Diego area. In the permanent collection are dinosaur and whalebones that delight kids of all ages.

With its Omnimax theatre, the Reuben H. Fleet Science Center, opened in 1973, is a great place for the whole family. The Fleet has exhibitions galore, many with the kids in mind, and a variety of Imax films to see each day. Visitors to the science center will also enjoy a simulated space flight in the Sci-Tours section.

From the Evenson Fountain the botanically minded might take the footbridge across Park Boulevard to view the superb cactus and rose gardens. From there it's a short walk south to the Centro Cultural de la Raza and the WorldBeat Center.

The colorful Centro is dedicated to preserving Chicano, Mexican, and Native American culture through art, music, dance, film, and education. And nearby, the WorldBeat Center strives to promote unity and diversity by expanding awareness and appreciation of the African Diaspora.

PYGMY SPERM WHALE

PYGMY SPERM WHALE
Kogia breviceps

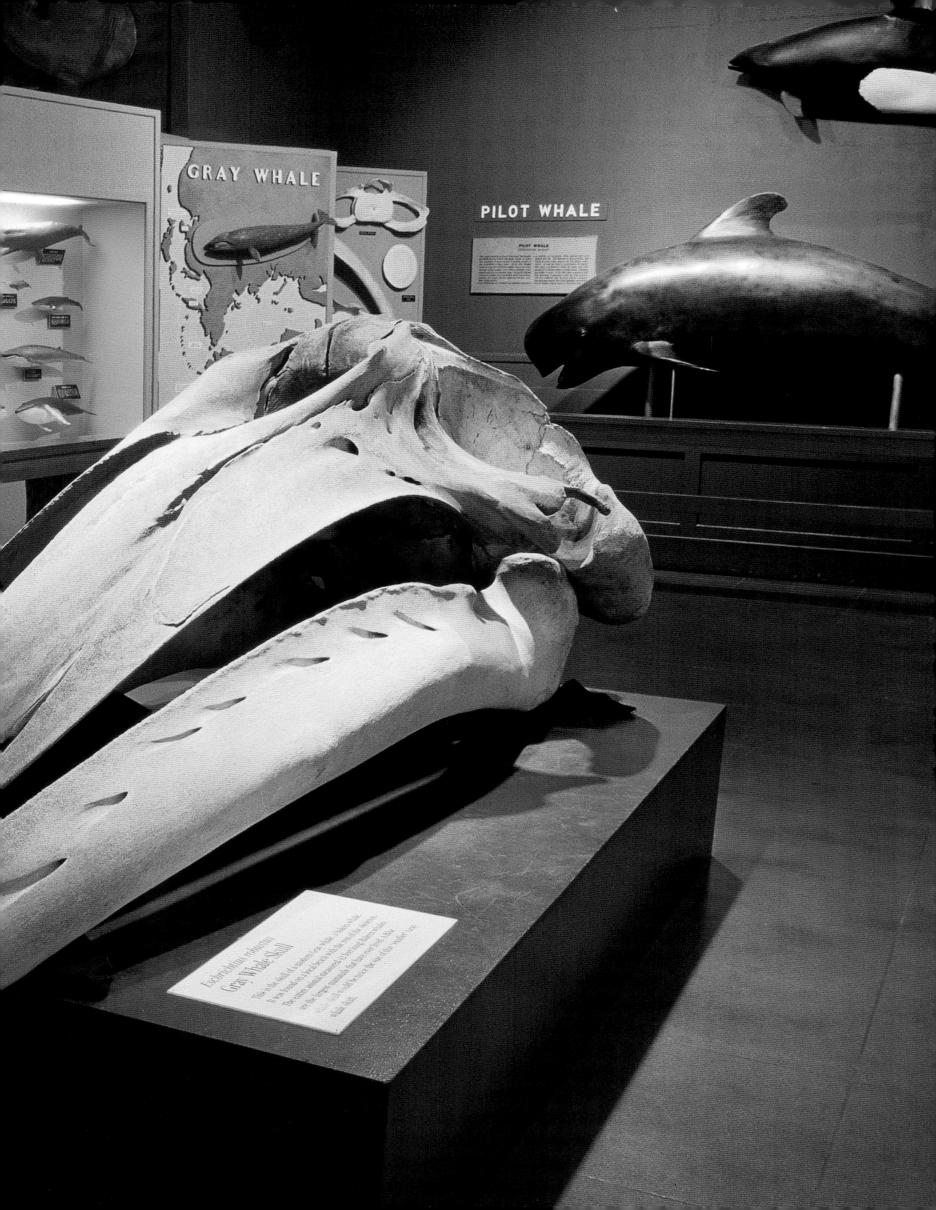

GRAY WHALE

PILOT WHALE

Eschrichtius robustus
Gray Whale Skull

Off Park Boulevard at Presidents Way, you will find Pan American Plaza, which hosts the San Diego Hall of Champions sports museum, the San Diego Automotive Museum, the Aerospace Museum, and the Starlight Bowl.

Having outgrown its former space on the Prado, the Hall of Champions moved into the remodeled 1935 Federal Building in 1999. In its three-level facility are special exhibits and a permanent collection, including an amazing interactive baseball exhibit. Located next to the baseball wing is an exhibit detailing the history of San Diego football. There is also a collection of works by noted sports sculptor A. Thomas Schomberg, including the original model for Rocky Balboa. Don't miss the tribute to San Diego baseball legend Ted Williams or the Breitbard Hall of Fame, named for museum founder and sports figure Bob Breitbard.

The Aerospace Museum is easily spotted. There's a Lockheed A-12 spy plane in its front yard. The exhibition areas present a chronological history of aviation and space flight. The museum details more than sixty-five American and foreign aircraft and spacecraft, including the first mail plane, World War II fighters, and modern-day jets. The Aerospace Museum has

its own Hall of Fame honoring the Wright Brothers, Amelia Earhart, and Wally Schirra.

Next to the Aerospace Museum is the Automotive Museum. Automobile lovers will find more than eighty vintage and classic cars, which make up the permanent collection. The museum also offers special exhibitions, ranging from horseless carriages to futuristic vehicles.

The Starlight Bowl is best known for its wonderful musicals that are presented on summer evenings. Because it presents the musicals under the Lindbergh Field flight path, producers have devised a stop-action plan. A spotter signals the conductor with yellow, red, and green lights. When a large plane approaches the stage, action is frozen and the music stopped.

Left: An original Lockheed A-12 spy plane welcomes visitors to the Aerospace Museum. *Below:* Vintage World War II aircraft are on permanent display at the Aerospace Museum. *Opposite Top:* Automobile lovers will find vintage and classic cars in mint condition at the Automotive Museum. *Opposite Bottom:* A concert at the Spreckels Organ Pavilion in the early 1920s.

When the green light goes on, the conductor raises the baton and the show resumes. Aficionados take it all in stride, setting up elaborate picnics on the grass prior to curtain. It's an immensely popular San Diego tradition.

If you proceed north, you will find the Puppet Theatre and the Balboa Park Club. Also nearby is the famous Spreckels Organ Pavilion, which was dedicated on New Year's Eve in 1914.

The pavilion's claim to fame is that is houses the world's largest outdoor organ, given to the city by John D. Spreckels and his brother, Adolph. Rain or shine, there is a free organ concert every Sunday at 2 p.m.

Just beyond the Organ Pavilion is the Japanese Friendship Garden and Tea Pavilion, a truly magical place. It is San-Kei-En, a garden of three scenes: mountain, water, and pasture. The garden contains a 12,000-gallon Koi pond replete with waterfall and a turtle island. There is also a wisteria arbor, numerous bonsai, and gentle walking paths.

Across the street is the wooden footbridge to the Alcazar Garden. Descend the wooden steps and enter Palm Canyon, one of the loveliest gardens in San Diego, which features fifty-eight species, some dating to the early 1900s when Kate Sessions held sway. There are more than 450 plants in the canyon, which has a wooden platform and comfortable benches, where one may sit and contemplate Balboa Park's beauty.

San Diegans had the vision long ago to set aside land for Balboa Park, which is certainly one of the most beautiful urban parks in the world. Today, that vision has become the heart of San Diego's cultural community.

San Diego
Nearby Attractions

WHAT SAN DIEGANS REFER TO as North County begins at Del Mar on the coast and extends north through the beach towns of Solana Beach, Cardiff-by-the-Sea, Encinitas, Leucadia, Carlsbad, and Oceanside. On the east, North County encompasses, among many others, the inland communities of Ramona, Julian, Rancho Bernardo, and Escondido.

where "the surf meets the turf." The Del Mar Thoroughbred Club was founded in 1936 and became a celebrity hangout for Harry James, Bette Grable, Bing Crosby, and Jimmy Durante. The racing season extends from late July to early September. The site is also used for the annual June-July San Diego County Fair.

North of Del Mar in Encinitas, Quail Botanical Gardens exists to conserve rare and endangered plants from around the world. Additionally, they ship tender eucalyptus clippings, the koala's favorite snack, to the San Diego Zoo. The Botanical Gardens flora is displayed in 24 beautifully arranged gardens that represent desert, tropical, subtropical, and Mediterranean climates. There's a rain forest, and one area is dedicated entirely to plants that are native to California.

Opposite: **Just another sunset in paradise.** *Top:* **Tropical vegetation like this bamboo can be found in abundance at Quail Botanical Gardens.** *Above:* **Locals at the Del Mar Racetrack claim it's "where the turf meets the surf."** *Right:* **Ballooning is a popular activity in San Diego's North County.**

The first town you reach when traveling north of San Diego is Del Mar, a largely unspoiled beach town with an especially dense sprinkling of shops and restaurants. Book lovers are urged to visit EarthSong Bookstore and Del Mar Plaza's Esmeralda, where one can grab a cup of java and a great sandwich.

Another favorite stop is the Del Mar Racetrack, known as the place

Also in Encinitas, extraordinary beauty and tranquillity are offered to those seeking peace at the Self-Realization Center, recognizable by its white façade, golden dome, and tall, mature palm trees. Paramahansa Yogananda established two Self-Realization Fellowship Ashram Centers in the San Diego area. The Encinitas locale was founded in 1937, and the second, located on First Avenue in San Diego, was established in 1943.

Just north of Encinitas in Carlsbad is another family favorite, Legoland, a 128-acre theme park with more than fifty rides, shows, and activities. Recently opened, Legoland is located in a former flower field and is one of four international Legoland parks, created for families with children 2 to 12 years old. Toddlers begin on Playtown and Legoland Express, then they move to Kid Power Tower, the Sky Cruiser, and finally, they may ride the Technic Coaster and the Dragon. To amaze and fascinate both kids and adults there are 5,000 models made from 30 million Lego bricks, plus a model shop where visitors can observe how it's done.

Located inland approximately thirty miles north of San Diego is Escondido, which was discovered by Spanish explorer Juan Bautista de Anza and was part of Rancho del Diablo, an 1843 Mexican land grant. The city of Escondido was incorporated two years later. The area is known for its rolling hills, citrus, grapes, avocados, wineries, and golf courses. Among its delights is Daley Ranch, a 3,039-acre conservation area run by the City of Escondido since 1997.

Hiking and mountain biking are quite popular. Also nearby is the Lawrence Welk Center, replete with memorabilia, guest accommodations, shopping, a musical theatre, and a golf course.

Comprising two excellent theatres and a museum and art gallery, the California Center for the Performing Arts, designed by Charles Moore, opened on twelve acres in the heart of downtown Escondido in 1994. The concert hall seats 1,538 and accommodates touring Broadway musicals, dance, symphony concerts, and recitals. The smaller 408-seat theatre is excellent for jazz, recitals, and plays.

Top: In the spring, fields of flowers in Carlsbad draw sightseers from across the State. *Above:* Escondido has an excellent climate for growing wine grapes. *Left:* A LegoLand worker puts the finishing touches on a miniature world. *Opposite:* A spectacular wildflower bloom, which peaks in February and March, follows winter rains in the Anza Borrego Desert State Park in eastern San Diego County. At more than 600,000 acres, visitors flock to California's largest state park to see the amazing colors. *Pages 58-59:* A surfer appreciates the final moments of daylight.

Escondido is also home to the San Diego Wild Animal Park, which is run by the San Diego Zoo. Opened in May 1972, it is dedicated to species preservation, breeding, and public viewing of animals in habitats very close to native. Visitors enter the park through an immense free-flight aviary. Not to be missed are the animal care center, the thirty-two-acre Heart of Africa walking safari, and a ride on the five-mile, fifty-minute Wgasa Bush Line monorail, from which you can view the animals of Africa and Asia roaming freely in natural herds and flocks.

The northernmost city you will come to is Oceanside. With a population of 160,000, it has much to offer in the way of scenic and historic delights. The 18th of the twenty-one California missions, Mission San Luis Rey de Francia was established in 1798. It is the largest working mission in California. Guided tours, a museum, a gift shop, and a Franciscan retreat center are located on the grounds, through which visitors are welcome to stroll.

Oceanside has the longest pier on the West Coast, and the adjacent beach offers a fine stretch of sand, fifty fire rings, and playground equipment. Truly a progressive city, Oceanside recently completed a fine civic center and library within walking distance of the Oceanside Museum of Art, which occupies the original, refurbished, Depression-era city hall designed by Irving Gill.

Among Oceanside's additional virtues is a one hundred-acre, 800-slip small craft harbor, which was constructed in the 1960s. The marina offers sport fishing, numerous restaurants, and waterfront accommodations. The secluded area feels as if it's a million miles from civilization— it's a great way to get away from it all, take in the sights, and just relax.

South of the Border

Located just twenty to thirty minutes south of downtown San Diego, Tijuana, Mexico is populated by an estimated 1.8 million people. The world's most visited border city, Tijuana is the gateway to the Baja peninsula. The city has long enjoyed the status of a playground and duty-free shopping destination, as more than 21 million tourists cross the border each year.

The cultural heart of Tijuana is Centro Cultural, which was built in 1982. The Cultural Center is known as CECUT or La Bola (the ball) and is dominated by a huge sphere that houses a planetarium and Omnimax theater. CECUT is also home to the Museum of the Californias; the Museum of Mexican Identities; an attractive, comfortable performing arts theatre that seats 1,100; a variety of shops; and a large restaurant.

While Centro Cultural is the heart of the city, most people actually go to Tijuana for the shopping, which is concentrated along Avenida Revolucion. Bargains abound and prices on high-end items such as perfumes, leather goods, furniture, and Mexican arts and crafts are typically forty to seventy percent lower than stateside.

Touted as the best shop in Tijuana, Bazar de Mexico is an 18,000 square-foot exposition hall showcasing individual artisans and their crafts, including papier mache corn husk flowers, pottery, blown glass, textiles, obsidian Aztec calendars, fine art, hand-carved furniture, wrought iron, silver and pewter, stained glass, Huichol Indian arts, Talavera pottery, and Tiffany-style lighting fixtures. For shoppers' convenience there is even a packing and mailing facility on site.

Restaurants are plentiful in Tijuana, but highly recommended are Carnitas Uruapan, which has the best mariachi music in town, and Casa del Mole, where the chicken can be ordered as you like it.

Bienvenidos, amigos!

Opposite: A giraffe family greets guests at the San Diego Wild Animal Park in Escondido.
Above: Shopping in one of Tijuana's upscale stores is a favorite pastime for many visitors.
Right: An African rhinoceros stands watch at the San Diego Wild Animal Park.
Pages 62-63: Fishermen take advantage of the fading daylight.

Acknowledgements

I would like to offer a special thanks to all my friends and family, the San Diego Historical Society, the Baja California Tourism Department, the Balboa Park Information Center, and the San Diego Convention and Visitors Bureau.

Resources

Balboa Park Visitors Center
1549 El Prado, Suite #1
San Diego, CA 92101
(619) 239-0512
www.balboapark.org

Bazaar del Mundo
2754 Calhoun Street
San Diego, CA 92110
(619) 296-3131
www.bazaardelmundo.com

Birch Aquarium at Scripps
2300 Expedition Way
La Jolla, CA 92037
(858) 534-FISH
www.aquarium.ucsd.edu

Cabrillo National Monument
1800 Cabrillo Memorial Drive
San Diego, CA 92106
(619) 557-5450
www.nps.gov/cabr/

California Center for the Arts
340 N Escondido Blvd.
Escondido, CA 92025
(760) 839-4138
www.artcenter.org

Chinese Historical Museum
404 3rd Avenue
San Diego, CA 92101
(619) 338-9888

Civic Theatre
202 C Street
San Diego, CA 92101
(619) 570-1100 (box office)

Copley Symphony Hall
750 B Street
San Diego, CA 92101
(619) 235-0804

Coronado Historical Society
1100 Orange Avenue
Coronado, CA 92118
(619) 437-8788
www.coronadohistory.org

Globe Theatres
1363 Old Globe Way
San Diego, CA 92101
(619) 231-1941,
Box Office (619) 239-2255
www.theglobetheatres.org

Heritage Park
2454 Heritage Park Row
Old Town San Diego,
CA 92110
(858) 565-3600

Holland America Line
300 Elliott Avenue West
Seattle, WA 98119
877-SAIL HAL
www.hollandamerica.com

Horton Grand Hotel
311 Island Avenue
San Diego, CA 92101
(619) 544-1886
www.hortongrand.com

Hotel del Coronado
1500 Orange Avenue
Coronado, CA 92118
(619) 435-6611
www.hoteldel.com

Japanese Friendship Garden
2215 Pan American Plaza East
San Diego, CA 92101
(619) 232-2780
www.niwa.org

Lamb's Players Theatre
1142 Orange Avenue
Coronado, CA 92178
(619) 437-6050
www.lambsplayers.org

Legoland California
1 Legoland Drive
Carlsbad, CA 92008
(760) 918-5346

Mingei International Museum
1439 El Prado
San Diego, CA 92101
(619) 239-0003
www.mingei.org

Mission San Diego de Alcala
10818 San Diego Mission Road
San Diego, CA 92108
(619) 281-8449
www.missionsandiego.com

Museum of Contemporary Art
700 Prospect Avenue
La Jolla, CA 92037
(858) 454-3541
www.mcasd.org

Museum of Photographic Arts
1649 El Prado
San Diego, CA 92101
(619) 238-7559
www.mopa.org

Oceanside Museum of Art
760 Pier View Way
Oceanside, CA 92054
(760) 721-2787
www.oma-online.org

Old Town Trolley Tours
(619) 298-8687
www.trolleytours.com

Qualcomm Stadium
9449 Friars Road
San Diego, CA 92108
(619) 641-3100

Reuben H. Fleet Science Center
1875 El Prado, Suite 5
San Diego, CA 92101
(619) 238-1233

San Diego Art Institute
1439 El Prado
San Diego, CA 92101
(619) 236-0011
www.sandiego-art.org

San Diego Aerospace Museum
2001 Pan American Plaza
San Diego, CA 92101
(619) 234-8291
www.areospacemuseum.org

San Diego Automotive Museum
2080 Pan American Plaza
San Diego, CA 92101
(619) 231-AUTO
www.sdautomuseum.org

San Diego Convention and Visitors Bureau
11 Horton Plaza
San Diego, CA 92101
(619) 236-1212
www.sandiego.com

San Diego Convention Center
111 West Harbor Drive
San Diego, CA 92101
(619) 525-5000

San Diego Historical Society
1649 El Prado
San Diego, CA 92101
(619) 232-6203

San Diego Maritime Museum
1492 North Harbor Drive
San Diego, CA 92101
(619) 234-9153

San Diego Museum of Art
1450 El Prado
San Diego, CA 92101
(619) 232-7931
www.sdmart.org

San Diego Museum of Man
1350 El Prado
San Diego, CA 92101
(619) 239-2001
www.museumofman.org

San Diego Hall of Champions
2131 Pan American Plaza
San Diego, CA 92101
(619) 234-2544
www.sandiegosports.org

San Diego Zoo
2920 Zoo Drive
San Diego, CA 92101
(619) 234-3153
www.sandiegozoo.org

SeaWorld, San Diego
500 SeaWorld Drive
San Diego, CA 92109
(619) 236-3901
www.seaworld.com

Theatre in Old Town
4040 Twiggs Street
San Diego, CA 92110
(619) 688-2494
www.theatreinoldtown.com

Tijuana Convention and Visitors Bureau
710 East San Isidro Boulevard, Suite 1165
San Isidro, CA 92173
(888) 775-2417

Torrey Pines Golf Course
11480 North Torrey Pines Road
La Jolla, CA 92037
(800) 985-GOLF

Torrey Pines State Reserve
Highway 101, Call for directions
(858) 755-2063
www.torreypine.org